Medieval World

TOWN LIFE

FIONA MACDONALD

A⁺
Smart Apple Media

First published in the UK by Franklin Watts
96 Leonard Street, London EC2A 4XD

Produced by Arcturus Publishing Ltd.
26/27 Bickels Yard, 151-153 Bermondsey Street, London SE1 3HA
Copyright © 2004 Arcturus Publishing Ltd.

Series concept: Alex Woolf
Editor: Clare Weaver
Designer: Chris Halls, Mind's Eye Design Ltd., Lewes
Illustrator: Adam Hook
Picture researcher: Glass Onion Pictures

Published in the United States by Smart Apple Media
2140 Howard Drive West, North Mankato, MN 56003

Library of Congress Control Number: 2004104270

ISBN 1-58340-570-4

9 8 7 6 5 4 3 2 1

Picture Acknowledgements: Akg-images, Vienna Austrian National Library 13; The Art Archive/Museo Storico
Topografico Firenze com'era Florence/Dagli Orti 4, /British Library 6, /Dagli Orti 7, /Museo Civico Bologna/Dagli Orti
8, /Bibliotheque Municipale Rouen/Dagli Orti 12, /Museo Civico Citta di Castello/Dagli Orti 17, /University Library
Prague/Dagli Orti 18, /Museo d'Arte Nazionale d'Abruzzo L'Aquila/Dagli Orti 20, /Issogne Castle Val'Aosta/Dagli Orti
(A) 21, /Museo Civico Bologna/Dagli Orti 25, /Real biblioteca de lo Escorial/Dagli Orti 27, /British Library 28, /Musee
Conde Chantilly/Dagli Orti 29; Bridgeman Art Library/Guildhall Library, Corporation of London, UK cover, 14,
/British Library, London UK 16, /Archives Charmet 24; Mary Evans 10; © 2001 Topham Picturepoint 22, / © Brian
Yarvin/The Image Works © 2003/Topham Image Works 23.

CONTENTS

TYPES OF TOWNS

Letter from King John of England to Families Wanting to Live in His New Town, Liverpool, 1207:

"The king to all who wish to have burgages [rent houses and shops] in the town of Liverpool, greeting. Know that we have granted to all who take up burgages at Liverpool that they shall have all the liberties [rights] and free customs [freedom to trade] as enjoyed by any other free borough on the sea-coast in our land. And so we command that you travel there safely and in our peace in order to receive your burgages and to live there."

A medieval town was a special place, separate from the countryside. Often, it was shut away from its surroundings behind strong gates and walls. People living in medieval towns had special, different jobs—making things to sell, working in shops or offices, or providing food and drink, lodging for travelers, or entertainment. These trades made medieval towns rich, interesting, and exciting. But they were also noisy, dirty, dangerous, and sometimes deadly places to live.

There were towns all over Europe, from northern Scandinavia to the southern shores of the Black Sea. They all had very different histories. Some, like Marseilles in France, Constantinople (Istanbul) in modern–day Turkey, and York in England, had survived from ancient Greek and Roman times. Others, like Winchester, in southern England, had been built as safe strongholds during the warlike years that followed the collapse of Roman power around A.D. 450.

The rich trading city of Florence, Italy, around 1490. Many fine churches, bridges, merchants' houses, workshops, and ordinary family homes are crowded inside its strong protective walls.

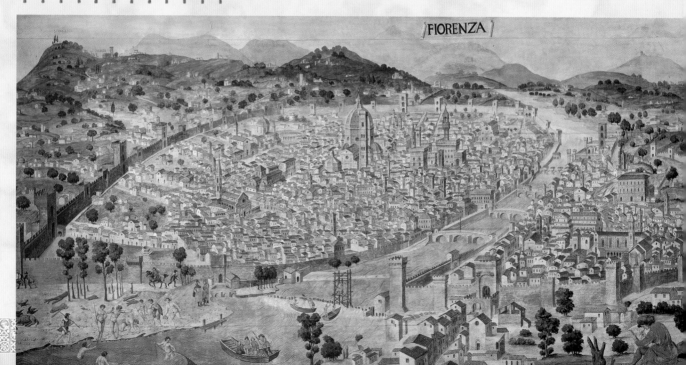

FIORENZA

Important towns of medieval Europe.

Some towns, like Aachen, in southern Germany, or Rheims in northern France, grew up between A.D. 500 and 1000, close to government headquarters or an important royal church, and shared in their prestige. But many of the richest towns, including Hedeby in Denmark, Dublin in Ireland, Bruges in Belgium, and London in England, developed as trading centers. They were close to safe harbors, beside busy long-distance tracks, or at river-crossings.

Many European towns were founded before A.D. 1000. But during the next three centuries, thousands of new towns, more than 125 in England alone, were created by powerful people such as bishops or kings. By founding them, they hoped to make money from renting town property and from collecting taxes on town trade. Some new towns were located next to lords' castles for protection, such as Edinburgh in Scotland; others were built close to sources of valuable raw materials. Freiburg, Germany (founded 1185), for example, is famous for its silver mines.

New-town building almost stopped after 1350. This was because Europe's population fell sharply as a result of famine and disease. In consequence, prices of everyday goods, such as food, that towns used to sell, also fell, along with lords' income from town taxes and merchants' profits. To try and survive, many towns changed their way of trading, producing fewer, but more costly, goods for wealthy people to buy.

Towns: Did You Know?
- Medieval towns and cities were big. The largest in western Europe (Paris, France) had more than 200,000 citizens in 1300.
- Most townspeople were women—and most of them were poor.
- Around one in three people living in towns was a servant.
- Townspeople could be fined for sheltering illegal immigrants from the countryside.
- Some cities in Italy, Germany, and Russia became so rich and powerful that they turned themselves into independent states and kingdoms.

WHO LIVED IN TOWNS?

Town Freedom

Medieval people had a saying: "Town air makes you free." An "unfree" peasant who ran away from a lord's estate and lived in a town for a year and a day could claim freedom, forever. He could also apply to become a burgess—if he managed to earn enough money to pay the joining fee, and he had friends among the existing burgesses to support his claim. Many poor people could not afford to become burgesses, so over the years, town communities became divided. A small, elite group of burgess families owned town property and ran town governments. Most other citizens were simply workers.

Historians estimate that about 20 percent—one in five—of the European population lived and worked in towns. Some people were born there, to long-established town families. Others made the decision to migrate to towns to make a new life, away from the countryside.

Unlike today, men and women who wanted to live in a nearby town could not just simply move there and be allowed to play a full part in town life right away. Town-dwellers—often called "burgesses" or "citizens"—had special rights and privileges, which they guarded jealously. For example, only they could own or rent houses and shops in a town, store their goods in its warehouses, or tie up their cargo ships in its harbor. Or they might be free from heavy taxes charged on goods brought by outsiders into town to sell.

Europe's first banks began business in towns. These late-14th-century illustrations show money-lenders, borrowers, and bankers.

In return for these rights, burgesses also had special duties—for example, not to shelter thieves and cheats, or not to give away the town's trading secrets. They also had to share the task of running the town's local government or choosing officials, such as a mayor and bailiffs, to do this for them. Only men could be full burgesses. Women shared in their husband's or father's rank—and wealth—but could not own own property or take part in town government.

Throughout the Middle Ages, towns grew in size as people migrated to live in them. People came for different reasons. Some were optimistic: they came to look for work or to learn a new skill. Others wanted to be free (see page 6) and hoped to make money. Some were serious professionals, such as priests, teachers, doctors, lawyers, and scribes, who set up schools, offices, and consulting rooms in many towns.

But many people coming to live in towns were driven by desperation, not hope. They included farm workers who had lost their land, homeless families, abandoned wives, poor widows, orphaned children, and injured soldiers. If they could not find work in the country, or get help from their friends and families, their only hope was to make their way to a town. There, they might survive by doing odd jobs or receiving charity.

Oath Sworn by New Burgesses of Ipswich, Eastern England, circa 1450:
"Hear this, you bailiffs, coroners, and portmen [town officials], and all other men present, that I shall henceforth be a true burgess and keep secret the counsels and private matters of the town and its Great Courts, and not discuss them. Nor shall I disguise the goods of any man as my own goods, so that the town shall not lose any right or profit. . . . And I shall also be obedient to present or future bailiffs. . . . And I shall also pay my fair share of taxes. . . . And I shall support and maintain the town . . . with my body, goods, and chattels . . . so help me God."

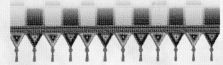

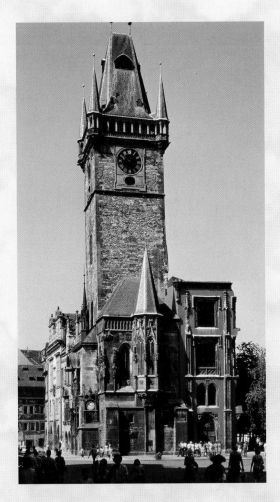

Local councils built grand meeting-halls to display their town's wealth and pride. This town hall, in Prague, Czech Republic, was built in the late 14th century.

7

MARKETS AND FAIRS

Trade was the most important activity in nearly every town. In the early Middle Ages, most trade took place at markets and fairs. These were both held regularly—markets once or twice a week, and fairs on holy days once or twice a year.

Customers trying on garments and buying lengths of fabric at the cloth market in Bologna, Italy, around 1450.

Description of the Great International Fair at Thessalonica, Greece, circa 1150:

"Not only do the inhabitants of that country [Greece] flock to it in great numbers, but multitudes also come from every race, including Russians . . . Italians . . . Spaniards, Portuguese, and French. What I saw there was a number of merchants' booths, set up in rows opposite each other. . . . There was every kind of material woven or spun by men or women . . . plus goods from nearby Greece and Macedonia, goods carried by ship from Italy, Spain, and Egypt, and Asian goods brought from Constantinople on horses and mules."

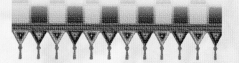

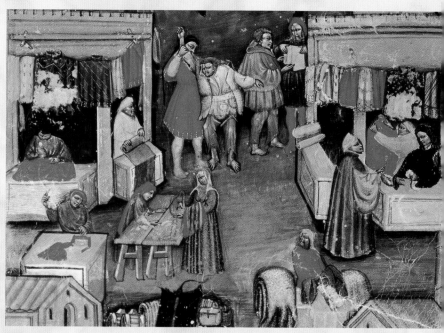

Markets sold everyday foods, such as fish and meat, butter, cheese and eggs, fresh fruit, vegetables, and herbs. Market stalls also sold useful items such as rough clothing, heavy leather shoes, farm tools, pottery, wooden bowls, and combs made of cow horn. Hungry customers could also buy fresh bread and beer, made by brewers and bakers in towns—and hot meat "coffyns" (pies), a favorite take-out snack.

Men and women walked or rode many miles into towns to bring goods to sell at markets, or to buy items they could not grow or make for themselves. Most villages had no shops, and markets also gave buyers the chance to see goods produced in different places throughout their local area. An ordinary villager could not possibly visit them all.

Medieval people looked forward to fairs as special occasions, where they could buy exotic goods, such as perfumes or spices, and meet traders from different lands. Unlike markets, which closed at the end of each day, a fair might last for a week or more. Traveling entertainers, musicians, sports matches, dancing, and even special religious processions all added to the fun.

The importance of trade was reflected in the layout of most European towns. At their heart, most had a large market-place for traders' stalls. In wealthy towns there might also be a covered market, sheltered by a wide roof, or a grand trading hall, where merchants could display valuable goods in comfort and safety. The marketplace would also have a cross or a saint's statue (to protect customers and traders) and an office for market officials. They checked weights and measures, and kept a lookout for counterfeit coins.

Fairs were usually located on the outskirts of a town, so traveling merchants would have plenty of space to set up their booths. Nearby, there would be grassland where they could park their carts and wagons, pitch their tents, and graze their horses.

Opportunities for Sin!
Medieval preachers did not like markets or fairs. They complained that markets were held on holy days, when traders should have been at church rather than in the marketplace, buying and selling. They also complained that trade provided too many opportunities for sinful behavior, such as swearing, boasting, lying, cheating, quarrelling—or drinking, to celebrate a bargain!

Market traders displayed goods made in family workshops—such as these leather jugs and shoes—on wooden stalls in open-air marketplaces. Cloth awnings sheltered traders and customers from rain and sun.

LARGE TOWNS AND CITIES

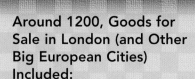

Around 1200, Goods for Sale in London (and Other Big European Cities) Included:
- gold from Arabia
- spices and incense from the shores of the Red Sea
- weapons from Scythia
- palm oil from Iraq
- gemstones from Africa
- silk from China
- wine from France
- furs from Russia and Scandinavia.

Trade created wealth, provided jobs, and encouraged the spread of new products, technologies, and ideas. It built up a network of contacts between different countries in medieval Europe, and between Europe and the wider world.

This international trade helped many of Europe's leading cities and towns grow very rich, and surprisingly big. The largest medieval city—Paris (France)—housed around 200,000 people in 1300. The next largest—Venice and Milan (Italy)—were home to more than 100,000 men, women, and children. Around 14 other cities, including London (England) Bruges and Ghent (Belgium), Seville and Cordoba (Spain), and Florence, Naples, and Genoa (Italy), all had between 50,000 and 100,000 inhabitants.

Ships at harbor in the busy port of London around 1500.

Long-distance trade relied on the sea. There were no planes, trains, trucks, or fast roads in medieval times, and ships were the best, and sometimes the only, way of transporting large loads over long distances. Almost all of Europe's great cities had thriving harbors, on the coast or beside wide rivers, where ships could tie up and unload. The wharves were lined with huge wooden cranes, to lift heavy goods from ships' holds into tall warehouses, where they could be safely stored. Many merchants had countinghouses (offices) close to the docks, where they could keep careful records of all their trade. Mayors and councils also built customhouses there, to collect taxes and tolls from foreign ships that wanted to trade in their cities.

The most profitable cargoes carried by medieval merchants were small, high-value items that could not be produced in Europe, or were specialities of just one region, such as Russian furs, or wool from eastern England and Spain. In the early Middle Ages, most Asian goods made part of their journey over land, across Asia, carried by camels over a network of tracks called the "Silk Road." But this route was blocked by Mongol armies from around 1306, so ships carrying Asian goods sailed across the Indian Ocean to ports in the Persian Gulf or Red Sea. Middle Eastern merchants took the goods to ports in the eastern Mediterranean and sold them to European traders, who then sailed back home.

Description of London by William FitzStephen, circa 1170:
"Among the celebrated and noble cities of the world, the city of London, the throne of the English kingdom, is more widely famed than any other, and sends its wealth and merchandise further afield. It is blessed in the strength of its defenses, the honor of its citizens, and the chastity of its wives. . . . [Its citizens] are known everywhere for the elegance of their manners, dress, and cuisine."

Traveling merchants—mostly from Muslim lands—led camels loaded with valuable goods from China through deserts and mountains along the Silk Road.

CRAFTS AND INDUSTRIES

As well as being busy ports and crowded trading centers, towns were also places where people made things. They had no big factories, like today's modern ones, where goods are mass-produced by machine. Instead, craftsmen and women worked at home, or in small workshops and studios, where they made all kinds of useful items by hand.

They hammered pewter to make jugs and dishes, melted wax and tallow to make candles, carved wooden furniture, knitted socks, designed hats and caps, wove twigs into baskets, mixed cosmetics and medicines, shaped delicate gold jewelry, or stitched fine embroidery. Craftwork was slow and painstaking, so craft goods could be expensive. Compared with today, most medieval people owned very few possessions, but they treasured them—usually, for life.

Advice [by a Woman Writer, (Christine de Pisan)] to Wives of Master-Craftsmen:
"If [you] wish to earn money honorably, urge your husbands and workmen to start work early, and keep working until late. Make sure you know the craft so well that you can organize the workmen if your husband is not there, or scold them if they do not work well. You must warn them against laziness. . . . Don't let unknown clients run up large bills. . . ."
(Adapted from A Medieval Woman's Mirror of Honor: The Treasury of the City of Ladies, *C. Willard and M. Cosman, trans. and ed.)*

Expensive luxuries for sale at a covered (indoor) market in France, around 1450.

A 14th-century tailor measures a customer before making a new robe. His apprentices (trainees) carefully sew clothes for other customers by hand.

Many town houses had a back room or a yard where family members and their servants worked. But some trades, such as blacksmithing, pottery, or glass-making, needed special equipment, including dangerous fires and furnaces. They were limited to certain streets of the town, where a careful watch could be kept to make sure that they did not set neighboring buildings on fire.

Other trades, especially tanning leather or dyeing cloth, were so smelly (both used stale urine in their work—it provided essential chemicals) that they were banned from the town center. Almost always, tanners and dyers had to work outside the city walls.

Raw materials for all of these industries had to be carried to workers and workshops. They came either from ships in town harbors, or from the countryside nearby. Shipping was big business in medieval times. Vast quantities of heavy, bulky goods, such as wood and stone used for building, had to be transported to towns on lumbering carts pulled by horses, oxen, or mules.

Similar carts were used to carry barrels of wine, salted meat, honey, or dried beans and peas from country farms to city shops, and sacks of freshly ground flour from windmills and watermills to bakers in busy towns. Huge bales of raw wool, or heavy hanks of ready-spun thread, had to be delivered to spinners and weavers, along with bulky bundles of feathers for mattress-makers. Haulers also had to handle more troublesome, living cargoes, such as the 50,000 sheep and 20,000 goats taken for sale to just one city (Florence, Italy) every year.

High Status Trades
All craftworkers were skilled, but some enjoyed higher social status than others. They made luxury objects for rich clients and used costly materials. These were the top trades in Paris, France, around 1400:
• goldsmiths
• embroiderers
• makers of fine armor
• tapestry weavers.

GUILDS AND APPRENTICES

Town trade, and all town craft manufacturing, was controlled by organizations called "guilds." There were two different kinds: merchant guilds and craft guilds.

Merchant guilds were groups of rich, powerful traders who worked with town governments to control trade in towns. They fixed the prices at which goods could be sold in their town's market, checked weights and measures, tried to stop members from cheating customers or failing to pay their debts, and did all they could to increase the fame and prosperity of their town.

Craft guilds were brotherhoods of skilled workers who joined together to maintain high craft standards, improve working conditions, and care for members (and their families) who were old or ill. They also provided training in each craft's special skills.

Prices, Wages, and Pensions
Craft guilds tried to control prices charged by their members, and wages paid to them. They also laid down rules for working hours. In London, for example, no guild member was supposed to work longer than 16 hours a day in the summer, or 12 hours in the winter. Guilds collected fees from members to pay for meeting halls, feasts, church services, and to help fellow workers. For example, it cost 3s 4d (about two weeks' wages) to join the carpenters' guild in London in the mid-14th century. The same guild paid a pension of 2d per day to sick members—about two-thirds of a normal day's wages.

(There were 240d [pence] in every medieval pound and 12d [pence] in every shilling.)

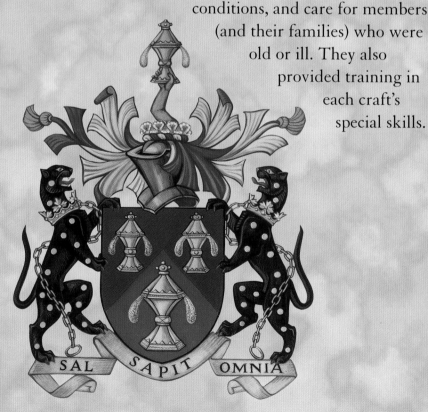

The coat of arms (official badge) of a medieval guild—the Salters Company of London, England.

SAL SAPIT OMNIA

A master stonemason watches while an apprentice practices his stone-cutting skills.

Training started at about 12 years old, when parents paid for a boy to become an apprentice. For the next two to seven years, he lived and worked with a master craftsman's family, learning all he could. He received food, clothes, and lodging, but no pay. At the end of his apprenticeship, he could join the craft guild as a "journeyman" (worker paid by the day). If he liked, he could leave the family who trained him and seek work elsewhere. Finally, when he felt confident of his skills, he could show a piece of his best work to senior members of the guild. If they approved this "masterpiece," he became a master craftsman. He could set up his own workshop, employ journeymen, and train apprentices of his own.

Girls could be apprenticed as well as boys. They usually trained at crafts such as embroidery or tailoring. Some women, like Mabel of St. Edmunds, in England, who made a robe for King Henry III around 1240, were highly praised— but they could not belong to any guilds. Full guild membership was for men only, although wives could be joint members with their husbands if they worked in the same family firm. A widow could also carry on her husband's business as if she were a guild member, but this was a special privilege. To help one another, some expert women workers in Paris (France) and Cologne (Germany) formed their own craft guilds, though these were never as powerful as the men's guilds.

Apprenticeship Agreement, Made in Marseilles, France, circa 1250:
" 'I, Peter Borre, in good faith and honestly, place with you, Peter Feissac, weaver, my son Stephen, for the purpose of learning the trade or craft of weaving, to live at your house and do work for you from the feast of Easter next for four continuous years, promising you by this agreement to take care that my son does the said work, and that he will be faithful and trustworthy in all that he does, and that he will neither steal nor take anything away from you, nor flee nor depart from you for any reason, until he has completed his apprenticeship. . . .'
'And I, the said Peter Feissac, promise you, Peter Borre, that I will teach your son faithfully and will provide food and clothing for him.' "

HOUSES AND HOMES

The Cost of Property in 14th-Century English Towns:

Yearly rent for three
London taverns £200 0s 0d

Yearly rent for 138 shops on
London Bridge £160 4s 0d

Yearly rent for a
merchant's house £3 0s 0d

Yearly rent for a journeyman's
house £1 0s 0d

Yearly rent for a
worker's house £5s 0d

Building a master goldsmith's
house, London £136 0s 0d

Building a merchant's
house £66 0s 0d

Building a journeyman's
house £15 0s 0d

Building a worker's
house £5 0s 0d

There were 240d (pence) in
every medieval pound and
12d (pence) in every shilling.
The average journeyman's
wage in the mid-14th century
was between 3d and 4d
per day.

The garden, complete with fountain, of a rich medieval house in Flanders (now Belgium) around 1500. In the background stands another fine town house, with a tall round tower.

Most cities and towns were surrounded by high wooden fences or strong stone walls, so building space inside was limited—and costly. This meant that visitors entering a medieval town found themselves in a very different environment from the surrounding countryside. Town streets were dark, narrow, and airless, and town houses were taller, narrower, and much closer together than country homes.

However, rich merchants' halls, or "palaces" as they were called in countries such as Italy, were very grand, with stone carvings or painted plasterwork, and comfortable, luxurious rooms for the family and its servants. They might also have a

This Italian painting, made around 1500, shows ordinary families' homes crowded side by side along a narrow, shadowy street.

...ounting house, and a showroom to display ...aluable goods for sale. Often, these fine homes ...ere built of brick or stone, and were protected ...rom the outside world by a high wall and ...netal-barred door, and guarded by a porter.

Town houses for ordinary families were built ...n very small plots of land. They were often ...oined to each other, in terraces (rows). If extra ...ooms were needed, for working, living, or ...torage space, houses were built two or more ...tories high. To create even more room, the ...pper rooms might jut out over the street ...elow. People also had a workshop or storage ...hed and a small yard at the rear. There might ...lso be a "backhouse"—a little hut over a pit of ...earth that was used as a lavatory.

Most ordinary homes were built of a timber framework ...with lath-and-plaster walls, and roofed with straw thatch ...or clay tiles.

Traders and craftworkers liked their homes to face directly ...onto the street so that they could use their front rooms as ...hops. Many houses had special shutters covering the front-...room windows that could be let down to form a shop ..."counter" where goods for sale could be displayed to passers-...by. Traders also hung brightly painted shop signs outside their ...homes—these had pictures of the goods produced, since most ...medieval people could not read. Families who worked in ...similar trades usually lived in the same street, which was ...named after them. There is still a street, for example, called ..."The Shambles" (which means "killing place") in York, ...England, where butchers used to live.

Comment by an Italian Visitor on the High Standard of Living in the Town of Nuremberg, Germany, Mid-15th Century:
"The citizens' houses seem to have been built for princes. In truth, the kings of Scotland [famous as a poor, wild country in medieval times] would gladly be housed so luxuriously as the ordinary citizen of Nuremberg."

FOOD AND DRINK

Town houses had no space for keeping animals, except, perhaps, a horse in a stable or a pig shut up in a small backyard sty. And there were few gardens, orchards, or fields inside town walls. So, town-dwellers had to rely on meat, fish, grain, fruit, and vegetables—and also olive oil, butter, cheese, and wine—produced by workers in the countryside or around the coast.

What people ate depended on how rich or poor they were. Rich families consumed large quantities of meat, which was often served in spicy sweet-and-sour sauces. They also liked white wheat bread—a medieval status symbol—sweet wine, and sugary treats such as marzipan.

In polite society, food was served in dishes called "messes," which were shared between two or four diners. People helped themselves from the "messe" with spoons or knives—forks were not yet widely used. At the start of a meal, each diner was given a thick slice of stale brown bread, called a trencher. People used this as a disposable plate. It held their food, and as they ate, fat and sauce soaked into it.

Customers waiting to buy fish at a busy Italian shop, around 1400.

Glutton (a Greedy Man) Visits a Pub in London, circa 1370:

"[Then] Beton the Brewer bade him good morrow. . . .
'I have good ale, friend,' she said, 'Glutton, will you try it?'
'Have you,' said he, 'any hot spices?'
'I have pepper and peony seeds,' said she, 'and a pound of garlic,
A farthing's worth of fennel seed for fasting days.'
Then Glutton goes in, and great oaths go with him.
Cesse the female cobbler sat on a bench,
Wat the warren-keeper and his wife both,
Tim the tinker and two of his lads,
Hick the horse-hirer and Hugh the needle-seller . . .
Sir Piers the priest and Pernelle of Flanders,
Davy the ditcher and a dozen others . . . [all]
gave Glutton with good will good ale as a treat."

Ordinary people ate large amounts of coarse brown bread; laborers consumed 5.5 pounds (2.5 kg) per day, or more! They also ate oat-cakes, barley bannocks, porridge, vegetable soup, peas, lentils, bacon (the cheapest meat), eggs, and whatever fruit and vegetables they could find. Men, women, and children mostly drank weak ale—this was sugary and starchy, and provided extra nourishment. Because ale was boiled during the brewing process, it was also safer than water to drink. To add interest to their plain-tasting meals, ordinary families added strong flavors such as pepper, garlic, and onions. The rich complained that working people stank of them!

Shopping, cooking, and serving meals was women's work, as was cleaning houses, washing clothes, caring for husbands and children, and entertaining visitors. Wealthy women had servants to do all of these tasks; women married to ordinary citizens, such as shopkeepers or journeymen, had to help in their husbands' businesses, too.

Providing food could also be a way for women to earn money. They brewed ale, ran public houses, cooked meals, or rented rooms to lodgers. Some women ran their own businesses, as food-sellers. They made luxury foods, such as fruit syrups and sweetmeats, to sell to rich customers, or bought perishable goods, such as milk, from country producers, to resell at higher prices in towns.

HEALTH AND WELFARE

Plague (Later Called the Black Death) in the Italian City of Siena, 1348:

"Father abandoned child, wife husband, one brother another . . . . None could be found to bury the dead for money or friendship. . . . They died by the hundreds, both day and night, and all were thrown in ditches and covered with earth. And as soon as those ditches were filled, more were dug. And I, Agnolo di Tura . . . buried my five children with my own hands."

Medieval towns were not very healthy places to live. Many managed to survive only because new settlers constantly arrived. They replaced existing citizens, who died more quickly, and at a younger age, than if they had been living in the countryside. Medieval people knew that they were taking a chance when they moved to a town, but many believed it was worthwhile. They either hoped to grow rich, or wanted to escape from a miserable existence in the country.

There were beggars in all medieval towns. Many of them were ill, or had disabilities. They could not find work and relied on charity to survive.

An Italian pharmacist mixing medicine, around 1450. Jars of herbs, spices, and chemicals can be seen on the shelves.

What killed townspeople? It was mostly dirt and disease. Town water was often polluted, and in homes without lavatories, people threw human waste into the gutter, or out of upstairs windows onto the street below. Horses and donkeys, used to pull carts, also created waste, which was often just piled up in the open air. Some town businesses, such as butchers' shops, produced smelly, rotting garbage that was a breeding ground for bacteria, rats, and flies.

In medieval times, people did not understand how bacteria caused dangerous illnesses such as dysentery and typhoid, which led to sickness and diarrhea, and killed many young children. (Around 4 of every 10 medieval babies did not reach the age of five.) They also did not know how rats, flies, and fleas passed on sickness. Rat-fleas were especially dangerous. From 1348 to 1350, their bites (which injected bacteria into the blood) spread an epidemic of a killer disease called plague. Overall, about one-third of the people in Europe died, the majority of them town-dwellers.

Homelessness, cold, and hunger were also serious problems in many medieval towns. Poor people usually slept in their employer's house—on the floor of the workshop, for example, or in a drafty attic. Out-of-work families found lodgings where they could. Sometimes, they rented a single room in a run-down, larger building. But often, they had to make do with temporary shelters in storage sheds, or slept in the open on the streets.

Public Healthcare
In the 15th century, many towns—led by Italian cities Milan and Venice—appointed special officials to safeguard public health. By 1450, the Milan team included:

- a physician (to prescribe medicines)
- a surgeon (to perform operations)
- a lawyer (to draft new laws)
- a barber (to let blood—believed to cure illness)
- two horsemen (for carrying urgent messages)
- three footmen (to be generally useful)
- two grave-diggers.

RELIGION IN TOWNS

Most people in medieval European towns followed the Christian faith. Some were devout. They worshipped God, prayed to the saints, and gave generously to charities. Others went to church on holy days but otherwise did not let their faith greatly affect their behavior. Many medieval people also believed in ancient, pre-Christian magic—such as witches who cast spells, ghosts who walked at Halloween, or spirits who lived in trees.

Whatever people privately believed, the Church as an institution was a powerful force in medieval towns. Church leaders had the right to summon men and women to church courts and punish them for breaking Church laws. The

Multicultural Life

There were communities of Jewish people living in many medieval European towns. In some places, like Italy, they lived and worked peacefully, as respected citizens. But in other countries, such as England, they were persecuted and eventually driven out. Until 1492, the south of Spain was governed by Muslim emirs (princes). In the early medieval era, they ruled over a brilliant multicultural civilization based in the city of Cordoba. Here, Muslims, Christians, and Jews from Europe, the Middle East, and North Africa created thriving businesses and great works of art and scholarship. But after around 1200, the south of Spain became a battleground, as Muslim and Christian rulers fought for control.

Controversial religious reformer Girolamo Savonarola attracted many followers in Florence, Italy. But his teachings were condemned by Church leaders, and he was executed in 1498.

This magnificent medieval cathedral towers over the city of Chartres, in France. It is now a world heritage site.

Church governed all kinds of personal behavior, such as telling lies, gossiping, swearing, sex before marriage, and adultery. The Church required everyone to make regular confessions of their sins to a priest, and it controlled ceremonies that marked the most important stages in people's lives, including baptism, marriage, and funerals.

The Church also had a powerful physical presence in towns. The largest, most beautiful town buildings—churches and cathedrals—belonged to it. They were built as centers of Christian worship, and to give glory to God. Some town churches and cathedrals were also places of pilgrimage. They housed relics (physical remains) of Christian saints. Thousands of pilgrims came each year to honor them, and to ask the saints for help—for example, to cure them from disease. After around 1300, many towns built huge churches where friars (missionary priests) preached rousing sermons to large congregations of ordinary citizens.

However, fine churches and cathedrals were also proud symbols of a town's wealth and status, and places where local craftworkers could display their skills. Leading families in many towns gave money to help build churches, and to construct family burial places and memorial statues inside them.

Town councils and church leaders often worked together to control town politics. Usually, they were on the same side, against criminals or protesters, but occasionally they became involved in bitter disputes. Church leaders were also of two minds about the morality of big business. They relied on rich merchants for donations, but they also disapproved of lending money at interest (which was how town bankers made their profits), and taught that "Trade can scarcely if ever be pleasing to God."

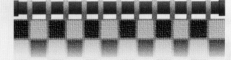

Advice from a 12th-Century Monk to a Rich Man:
"These soldiers of Christ [monks] fight very hard against the Devil. Who can count all the different hymns, psalms, prayers, and daily church services which monks perform? Therefore, powerful man, I strongly advise you to build a fortress [that is, a monastery] on your lands, as a base from which these soldiers of Christ can fight against the Devil, and offer their long, painful hours of prayer to please God."

BODY AND SOUL

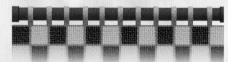

Some Famous Medieval Hospitals

- Hotel Dieu (God's House), Paris, France
  Founded 651
  300 beds
- St. John's Hospital, Bruges, Flanders
  Founded circa 1150
  75 beds
- San Spirito (Holy Spirit) Hospital, Rome, Italy
  Founded 1198
  300 beds
- Santa Maria Nuova (New St. Mary's) Hospital, Florence, Italy
  Founded 1288
  220 beds
- The Great Hospital, Norwich, England
  Founded 1245
  30 beds

(The numbers of beds refer to the 14th century.)

Nuns (in black) and their helpers (in white) care for sick and dying people at the Hotel Dieu (House of God). This was one of Europe's first-ever hospitals, founded by the Church soon after 600, in Paris, France.

The influence of the Church in towns extended far beyond religious duties. Many religious men and women dedicated their lives to "good works" and helped people living in towns in several different, important ways.

Monks and nuns ran hospitals. These were paid for by wealthy religious leaders or pious rich people who left gifts of land or money in their wills. They were staffed by lay brothers and sisters (men and women who had not made religious vows but wanted to work for the Church), who did most of the everyday nursing care.

Medieval hospitals could not cure many diseases. But, like modern hospices, they cared for people who were dying, or suffering from chronic (long-term) illness. Monks, nuns, and lay staff kept patients as clean and comfortable as possible, and tried to ease their pain. They also offered spiritual comfort—medieval people believed that making a "good death," blessed by the Church, was important—and promised to give them a religious burial.

Priests, monks, and nuns were the best-educated people in medieval society. They trained young people who joined their communities, and also other girls and boys who came to schoolrooms in town churches and cathedrals. Pupils learned to read and write Latin—the language used by scholars throughout the Christian world. They were also taught about theology (the study of religion), philosophy (the study of ideas), math, music, and rhetoric (how to organize their thoughts when writing, debating, or speaking in public).

Emperor Frederick II Sets up a University in Naples, Italy, 1224:

"We wish that in all parts of the kingdom many people will become wise and knowledgeable, by having access to a fountain of knowledge, a garden of teaching, so that, once they have become clever by study and observation, they will serve God's justice, and become useful to us, and our government. . . . We have therefore decided that in the most pleasant city of Naples there should be teaching of the arts and all subjects, so that those who are starved of knowledge will find it."

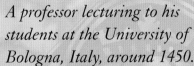

A professor lecturing to his students at the University of Bologna, Italy, around 1450.

The most learned priests and monks were recruited to teach at new universities, set up in big cities all over Europe from around 1200. (Women could not teach or study there.) Like hospitals, universities were paid for by wealthy people, who believed that education would benefit society. Students came there to study from miles around.

ENTERTAINMENT

Medieval townspeople worked hard, but they also enjoyed many days off, when they could relax with their friends, neighbors, and families. Originally, most of their holidays were Church festivals (the word "holiday" comes from "holy-day"), such as Christmas, Easter, and saints' days. The Church hoped that men and women would use this time for prayer and religious study, but holidays soon became a time for entertainment of a nonreligious kind as well.

Many towns had their own special patron (protective) saint, whom they honored with elaborate church services and grand outdoor events. These often began solemnly, with processions of chanting priests carrying the saint's statue through the streets, and ended with rowdy behavior at sports contests such as the daring Palio horse-race in Siena, Italy, or bull-running in Pamplona, Spain. Many families also enjoyed picnics, or drinking parties at town inns.

At Christmas time, groups of actors, called mummers, put on masks and monster costumes, sang and danced, fought mock battles, and performed plays based on exciting stories from saints' lives (such as St. George killing the dragon), or ancient legends about mysterious nature-spirits, such as the Green Ma

Mystery Plays

In English, French, and German towns, favorite forms of entertainment included "mystery plays," performed by members of craft guilds. In spite of their name, they were not detective dramas. They were named after the French word for skilled trade, which was *métier*. Mystery plays grew out of earlier medieval dramas, performed in churches. They retold Bible stories but set them in the everyday medieval world, so ordinary people could understand their message— and enjoy them.

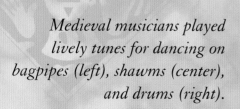

Medieval musicians played lively tunes for dancing on bagpipes (left), shawms (center), and drums (right).

Old, pre-Christian festivals were also celebrated in many towns; for example, by decorating houses with green garlands on May Day, and lighting bonfires at Midsummer.

Throughout the year, citizens looked forward to regular visits from traveling entertainers. These included jugglers, acrobats, animal-trainers, and fools—who told rude jokes and mocked powerful people. Musicians performed songs and dance tunes on fiddles, bagpipes, nackers (small drums), shawms (very loud reed instruments, like oboes), or the pipe-and-tabor. This was an early kind of one-man band. It consisted of a pipe, on which tunes were played with the left hand, and a flat drum, hit with the right hand.

English Workman, Reported (Disapprovingly) by a 12th-Century London Priest:
"When we workers have made enough money to buy food—with a bit left over, so we can have a drink, as well—then what we want to do is have a day off, and enjoy a good time, singing and dancing. We don't want your church services, your rotten old hymn tunes, or your saints. Just leave us alone."

Spanish noble ladies playing chess, 1282. They are sitting in an elegant building decorated in Spanish Muslim style.

Less-active amusements all year round included board games such as chess, and playing cards (both introduced to Europe by Muslims) and dice. Medieval people liked to bet on these, and also on wrestling matches, bear-baiting (fights between fierce dogs and bears), and matches between fighting cocks. (Most people today would find these last two forms of entertainment very bloodthirsty and cruel.)

27

TOWN TROUBLES

The biggest threat to any town was attack by enemies. Strong walls and gates could keep out enemies, but towns were still in danger of being besieged. During a siege, hostile troops camped outside a town, surrounded its walls and gates,

Medieval soldiers besieging a town, around 1450. They are armed with longbows and cannons.

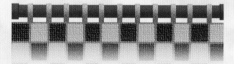

Town Punishments

"If bakers and brewers break the Assize of Bread and Beer [laws about weights, measures, and quality] one, two, or three times, they shall be fined. But if they go on breaking the law, then a baker shall be put in a pillory, and a brewer in a tumbrel."

Pillory: a tall wooden frame that was fixed around the neck and hands. Law-breakers were locked in the pillory, and townspeople threw rotten food and other garbage at them.

Tumbrel: a wooden sledge, or low cart with wheels. Law-breakers were tied onto this and dragged roughly through the streets, while townspeople jeered at them.

and refused to let anyone in or out. Eventually, all food in the town was eaten, and citizens starved. At the same time, enemy soldiers used massive "siege engines," such as battering rams, to try and smash through castle walls, shot spears and arrows at town defenders, and hurled dead bodies back into the town, to spread grief and fear. After around 1400, they also used cannons that fired iron shot to attack town walls.

Town treasures, such as gold crosses in churches, fine furnishings in merchants' houses, or valuable goods in warehouses, were all rich pickings for invaders. On many occasions, army leaders were unable to control their troops once they had forced their way into a town. Soldiers looted all they could, destroyed all the rest, and brutally attacked peaceful citizens.

because of these dangers, even in peace-time, all "foreigners" (noncitizens) had to identify themselves to guards on duty at town gates and give a good reason for wanting to enter the town. Town gates were kept locked from dusk to dawn, and councils imposed a curfew. This meant that no foreigner was allowed out of his house after dark—on threat of being arrested as a spy.

Town councils also worried about rowdy protests by young apprentices, complaining about low pay and poor working conditions, and violent riots by poor people, who resented the vast gap between them and the richest citizens of the town. Councils appointed watchmen to patrol the streets and keep a lookout for trouble, and they set up community-based schemes to report criminals, such as pickpockets, burglars, and confidence tricksters, who found many victims in towns. They held courts to try all of these offenders, and also to punish traders who damaged the town's good name by cheating customers.

Today, most towns built during the Middle Ages are still busy and thriving. But now they have street lights, paved roads, traffic, and high-rise buildings—and they are almost all much larger than they were 500 years ago. In spite of this, many features of medieval town life still survive today. There are still town mayors and town councillors, open air markets, streets lined with shops, fine town houses, and crowded slums. In some parts of Europe, medieval towns have been carefully preserved, as heritage centers and tourist attractions. People can still see their churches, merchants' homes, city walls, and narrow, winding streets and feel what it was like to live in medieval times.

Laws of Maldon, Essex, 1468:

- Every foreigner must be indoors by 10 P.M. in summer and 8 P.M. in winter.
- The bailiffs (town council officers) will punish all "naughty brawlers."
- If one man attacks another and draws blood, he will be fined.
- No foreigner shall carry a weapon in the town.
- Anyone who puts dung or trash on the public road shall be fined.
- Any pig wandering loose in the streets may be caught and sold, and the money will go to the town.
- Any councillor who stirs up quarrels at council meetings will be fined.
- No burgess may call a council officer "thief, knave, back-biter, whoreson [son of a prostitute], false, forsworn [breaker of promises], cuckold [man whose wife is unfaithful] or bawd [immoral]."

The Doge (elected ruler) of Venice, Italy, discusses city politics with top churchmen, while scribes (trained writers) make a careful record of their words.

TIMELINE

330	Roman empire divides. Constantinople (now Istanbul) becomes capital and grows into the greatest city in Europe.
476	Last Roman emperor leaves Rome.
c. 600–700	New trading towns ("wics") set up on either side of North Sea.
750	Vikings set up trading post at Staria Ladoga (now in northern Russia).
794	Frankish Emperor Charlemagne reforms coins, weights, and measures throughout his empire, to encourage trade.
822	Two cities, Novgorod and Kiev, unite to form first Russian state.
849–99	King Alfred the Great of Wessex, England, builds burghs (fortified towns) to defend his kingdom.
c. 1000	Cordoba, in Muslim Spain, is a great multicultural center of art, trade, and learning.
c. 1075–1122	Italian towns win right to govern themselves.
c. 1100–1300	The Church builds hospitals in towns; town councils make laws to improve cleanliness and public health.
c. 1160	Northern European cities build churches and cathedrals in soaring Gothic style.
c. 1175–1250	Great age of international trade fairs in Champagne region, France.
c. 1200–1500	Universities built in many European towns.
1204	Venice, Italy, controls shipping and trade in Mediterranean Sea.
1252	Rich Italian city of Florence makes first gold coins in almost 500 years—a sign that trade is flourishing.
1259	Northern European trading towns on shore of Baltic Sea join together in a powerful "Hansa" (league).
1265	Representatives of boroughs (towns) become members of English parliament.
1277–95	King Edward I of England founds 10 new towns in Wales, to control conquered land.
1277	Genoa, Italy, sets up trading route between Mediterranean and North Sea.
1309	First town clock in Europe, in Milan, Italy.
c. 1340	Around 15 cities in Europe now have more than 50,000 inhabitants.
1347–51	Black Death kills around one-third of Europe's population. Temporary collapse of trade.
1420–1600	Italian cities rebuilt in splendid Renaissance style.
1445–55	First Bible printed, in city of Mainz, Germany.
1453	Constantinople conquered by Muslim Ottoman Turks.

GLOSSARY AND FURTHER INFORMATION

apprentice A trainee craftworker.

bailiffs Officials employed by town governments.

bear-baiting Fighting between a bear and fierce dogs.

borough A large town, with its own government and market or fair.

brawler A fighter.

burgage House and shop in a town.

burgess A town-dweller who has rights to own property and take part in trade.

chastity Modest, moral behavior.

chattels Small, portable belongings.

chronic Long-lasting.

cobbler Maker and mender of shoes.

coroners Kings' officials who investigated suspicious deaths.

counsels Private information.

cuisine Cookery.

ditcher A road-worker.

fennel An herb that tastes of aniseed.

Flanders A region in northern Europe, now part of Belgium.

fool An entertainer who told rude jokes and made fun of important people.

free customs Freedom to trade.

friars Missionary priests.

interest Fee charged by people who lend money.

journeyman A trained craftworker, employed by the day.

lay brothers and sisters Men and women who were not monks or nuns, but who worked full time for the Church.

liberties Rights.

masterpiece An item of craftwork designed to show the maker's skills and to prove that he was good enough to work as a master craftsman.

mayor The leader of town government.

midden Trash heap.

mystery plays Dramas performed by townspeople, acting out stories from the Bible.

nackers Small drums.

peony A flowering plant.

philosophy The study of ideas.

rhetoric How to organize thoughts and ideas when speaking in public.

Scythia A region in Central Asia, to the northeast of the Black Sea.

shawm A very loud reed instrument, rather like an oboe.

tallow Sheep fat.

tanning Soaking, cleaning, and scraping the hair off hides, then treating them with mixtures of chemicals to turn them into leather.

theology The study of religion.

tinker A mender of metal pots and pans.

tolls Money charged for permission to trade in towns.

trencher A slice of stale bread used as a disposable plate.

warren-keeper A rabbit-keeper.

RECOMMENDED READING

Clare, John D. *Fourteenth-Century Towns.* New York: Harcourt, 1996.

Eastwood, Kay. *Medieval Society.* New York: Crabtree Publishing Co., 2003.

Grant, Neil. *Medieval Europe.* Mankato, Minn.: Smart Apple Media, 2003.

Macaulay, David. *Castle.* New York: Houghton Mifflin, 1983.

RECOMMENDED WEB SITES

http://www.msu.edu/~georgem1/history/medieval.htm
http://georgetown.edu/labyrinth/
http://www.learner.org/exhibits/middleages/

INDEX